Modernizing Markham

Bringing *The English Housewife* to Today's Readers

Julia Skinner

University of Iowa Center of the Book
Florida State University School of Library
& Information Studies

A Modern Markham Edition from
Candle Light Press
Iowa City, IA

To my uncle David Huntley.
Thank you for inspiring my love of food &
cooking, and using them to bring people
together. I miss you every day.

THE ENGLISH HOVSE-VVIFE.

CONTAINING

The inward and outward Vertues which
ought to be in a compleate Woman.

As her skill in Physicke, Surgery, Cookery,
Extraction of Oyles, Banqueting stuffe, Ordering of
great Feasts, Preseruing of all sorts of Wines, Conceited Secrets, Distillations, Perfumes, ordering of Wooll,
Hempe, Flax, making Cloth, and Dying, the knowledge of Dayries, office of Malting, of Oates,
their excellent vses in a Family, of Brewing, Baking, and all other things
belonging to an Houshold.

A Worke generally approued, and now the fourth time much
augmented, purged and made most profitable and
necessary for all men, and the generall good
of this Kingdome.

By G. M.

LONDON.
Printed by *Nicholas* Okes for John Harison, and are to
be sold at his shop at the signe of the golden
Vnicorne in Pater-noster-row. 1631.

Title page for The English Housewife, 1631 edition.

i

Table of Contents

Preface

This book represents a multifaceted project and a period of my career that I'm particularly proud of. As you will learn more about later on, the Markham project began as a class paper before turning into a draft of a journal article, and later my final project for my Center for the Book certificate. Projects that evolve and pull from multiple disciplines are ones that I tend to get the most excited about.

It is also special to me because of all the things I learned. This project allowed me to use and develop strengths in a number of areas and pull them together into a cohesive whole. It also gives me something great to talk about at parties, but the greatest lesson I've learned from Modernizing Markham is that academic work can be interdisciplinary, broadly focused, and (most of all) fun. I have seen quite a few research projects that effectively harness digital technologies to talk about phenomena online and off, and I am hoping that I can continue to blend old and new technologies and approaches throughout the rest of my career.

I also learned that everything is a work in progress, and that sometimes it's hard to consider a particular project "done." Hand in hand with that discovery was the discovery that you can bring a project to a successful conclusion even if there were things within the project that weren't flawless. For example, a few of the recipes just would not turn out. Some of it was user error (which will certainly improve as I continue to hone my skills) and some of it was the fact that the ingredients we rely on have changed over the centuries. I am still in the process of perfecting those recipes, and will continue to share my efforts with them and with new recipes on the Markham website. However, that desire for completion is why the book is being released without the failed recipes being perfected. The process of cooking is very similar to the process I engage in when making visual (inedible!) art: I never know how long it will take, and only sometimes know exactly what it will look like when I am finished. The project was successful, fun, and inspirational for me even with the stumbling blocks I encountered, and I want to share the book as a reflection of that process. As I write future recipes and as my skills and knowledge continue to grow, other books might emerge that are more technical or that are tested to death until every recipe I ever considered including is perfect, but at this moment I am content with this book and grateful that my publisher is as excited about it as I am.

I also learned from Markham himself. Markham was a character who lived in changing times and whose family's social standing was on the decline (you will read more about that later). Even though little evidence exists that helps me really understand Markham (although Michael Best does an incredible job with what is available), I feel like I can relate to him in some way. Markham was old-fashioned, and encouraged his readers to be frugal and eat inexpensive, wholesome foods at a time when other authors were sharing more banqueting and special occasion dishes. Markham's book feels more comfortable to me: the sort of book you engage with every day, as opposed to one you only pick up when panicking about what to make for company. I see Markham as a kindred spirit because he relies on simple, traditional foods, but balances his love of the old with his ability to harness new technologies and to share his breadth of knowledge (Markham published books on a variety of topics beyond cookery). I have often felt that I have one foot planted in history and tradition, and one in the modern day as I conduct historical research and produce art using historic techniques, while also researching internet use and social media.

Working with Calligraphy

As a part of the Modernizing Markham project, I thought it would be fun to play with historic book technologies in addition to the digital technologies that dominated the earlier parts of the project. To do this, I decided I would create a book that used materials and techniques that would have been used in manuscript books (rather than printed books) during Markham's time. I acquired some vellum and some paper that is similar to that used in the early modern period (the University of Iowa Center for the Book makes some very good papers for this purpose), and some walnut ink (which is not historically accurate, but which eats away at the paper less than more acidic gall-based inks).

In order to write the book the way I wanted to, I needed to use secretary hand, which was the style of writing in use when The English Housewife was published. Secretary hand evolved from styles of handwriting used in the Middle Ages, and was commonly used in Tudor England (Parkes, 1959). The style was not always consistent, making it difficult at times to read some letterforms. As with any style of writing, it required training to master, which accounts for some of this inconsistency and for some manuscripts written in an "inexperienced" hand (Wolfe, 2007). Handwriting also evolved over time, resulting in distinct letterforms produced by an individual over the course of his or her life (Ioppolo, 2006).

It also was a hand used by professionals during this period, and received its name because it was used in the Tudor period by royal secretaries, and was one of a number of handwriting styles created for particular types of texts. As a hand used in professional documents, it was mostly taught to men, while Roman and Italian styles were more often taught to women as they were thought to be appropriate for the occasional (non-professional) writing women engaged in (Ioppolo, 2010). Elizabeth I used an Italian hand in letters, but used those letterforms mixed with Secretary hand when producing official documents (Kinnamon, N. J., 2008). Secretary hand was used by professional scribes, who were trained to write in a uniform hand in order to produce high-quality documents. The hand has also been found in manuscripts by a number of literary and dramatic authors, although the quality of the writing varies greatly as these compositions were not produced by scribes. These literary and artistic works would also include multiple hands (e.g. italic and secretary) to denote different parts of a script (Ioppolo, 2006).

I started by looking around for ductus (or visual directions for drawing calligraphic letterforms) for handwriting that was used during Markham's time. I assumed that a set of instructions was already in existence (I later learned that Grace Ioppolo provides in-depth discussion and visual examples in her 2010 work), but at that time I could not find exactly what I needed in either print or online resources, and so decided I would create my own ductus. I studied historic examples, making a point to focus only on those created around the time The English Housewife was published (roughly twenty years before and after). I looked for common characteristics between those hands, and used what I had learned from my calligraphy instruction to think critically about the letterforms I was looking at (e.g. what is the dominant shape? Are the letters more tall and narrow or short and squat? How much space is there between letters?) Then, I practiced writing out letters that used the common characteristics I saw until they resembled the letters from the historic samples.

Based on my practice writing, I was able to reverse engineer my writing in or-

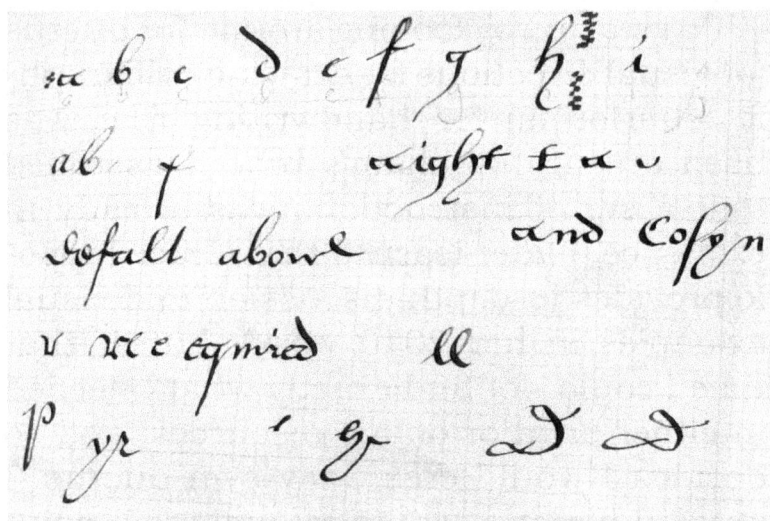

der to draw up ductus that others could use. I looked at each pen stroke I made and the direction it went, and then drew arrows corresponding to those strokes within the structure of the letters so others could replicate it (for an example, see the second line in the image below). As a part of the exhibit that accompanied this project, I drew up a poster with the ductus and the finished letterforms, and have published photos of it on my Flickr account so others can recreate the letters in their own work.

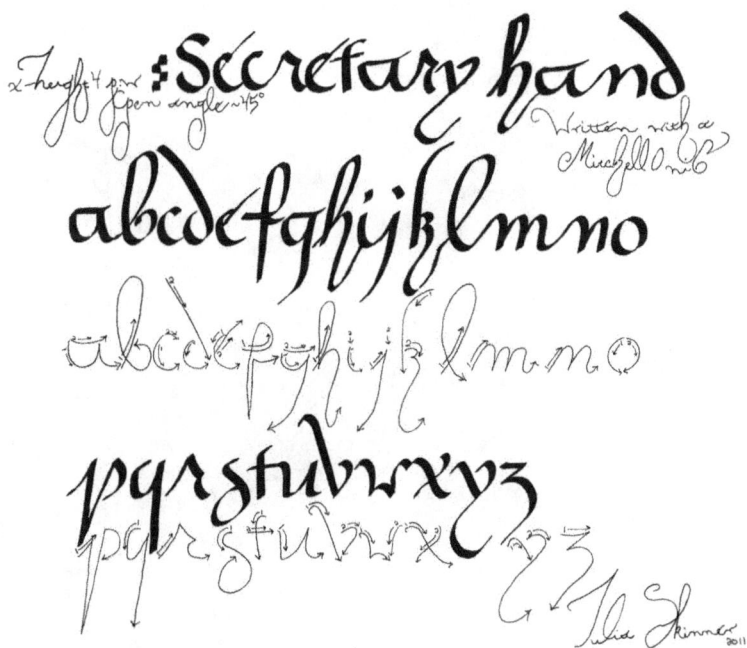

I have continued to practice the hand in my spare time, and it appears in other pieces of my artwork. As a result of this, the hand I used to match historic samples is slightly different than my own style, which has developed as time has progressed. In my own style, the ascenders and descenders are a little bit longer, and the letters a bit wider than in my original early drawings.

Introduction

Gervase Markham (1568-1637) was a prolific writer, producing dozens of works on running a middling country household for both men and women, along with some works of fiction (Best, xv-xvi). *The English Housewife* was first published in 1615, with a second edition published in 1623 (Best, xvii). Markham indicated that the book was simply a compilation of material from elsewhere, possibly from a noblewoman, rather than a work consisting of entirely new material (Best, xv-xvi). Printed cookbooks like Markham's were notable because many people at the time were still using manuscript cookbooks as references. His exploration of new media in his own work was an inspiration for the Modernizing Markham project, which combined social media with more traditional paper-based creative work.

Modernizing Markham was a multifaceted project created with the aim of making 17th-century recipes accessible to modern cooks, while placing Markham's work within the context of culinary history and book history. The first element was a blog, where recipes were posted and where resources were shared with readers. The blog will remain available online, free of charge, at http://modernizingmarkham. com. The goal of this approach was to reach as wide an audience as possible by writing in a way that avoided jargon or assumed specialist knowledge. This was facilitated by social media both through the project Twitter account (@ModernMarkham) and the author's personal Facebook and Twitter accounts (@BookishJulia).

The project also included a handmade book containing the modernized recipes. This book was pamphlet-bound using historically accurate materials, and calligraphed in a contemporary hand called secretary script. The handmade book was included as another exploration of multiple formats: it was reminiscent of the manuscript books still popular in Markham's day, but it also bears resemblance to modern handwritten books by Mollie Katzen, whose book pages have been handwritten and illustrated, rather than relying on fonts and designs that are consistent across pages. Being able to explore a single topic as it was embodied in different media, while using digital media to increase the topic's visibility, spoke to my interests as an artist and an editor.

As an information professional and former editor at an open access journal (http://ir.uiowa.edu/bsides), I am interested in how we can make scholarly research more accessible and interesting to the general public. Modernizing Markham was an attempt to make the content of a historic book relevant to modern readers, and put it in an interactive format that would draw a wider audience. The subject matter itself is also of interest to me, and is something I had worked on for quite some time. I began my fascination with Markham when writing a class paper. After adapting the paper as a journal article, I decided I wanted to go in a different direction with the research and share my knowledge of cooking and of Markham's work in a new way. I had the opportunity to use this as the basis of my Center for the Book final project, and decided that would be an excellent way to explore different possibilities under the guidance of knowledgeable historians and artists.

This project was important to me because it not only allowed me to share my knowledge to the reader, but allowed readers to interact with me and discuss history and recipes with each other on the blog. This feedback made the research process a collaborative effort and gave me the chance to explain my work to people who would ask about it online and in person. This approach also promoted understanding of the cookery manual as something that could be relevant today as an instructional text as well as an object of historical study. Books on healthy eating and the role of the diet in overall wellness are published to this day. While the content of the recipes has changed, Markham's book was also a product of a time when food was viewed as medicine, and eating well was a way to ensure health and longevity. By placing these recipes in a context modern readers can understand, it becomes easier to engage in a discussion about how our ideas of food's role in health maintenance have changed (and stayed the same).

Testing the recipes gave me a chance to learn how women in Markham's time interacted with food. While I made use of modern appliances and indoor plumbing, I tried to keep the recipes as true to the originals as possible. In most cases, adapting the recipes was relatively easy, although once in a while I had to spend a good deal of time considering how a recipe could be adapted without altering the finished product. In one case, the recipe for wafers, there was no option but to purchase a specialized tool for the recipe. In another instance, after three attempts to create Markham's Paste of Genoa (see Best, 116) I was still unable to reproduce the recipe. I had purchased apples that were small and firm, in the hopes they would be closer to those available in the seventeenth century. The apples resulted in two failed recipes, as did a later attempt with pears, indicating that there is something about modern fruit that differs enough to make certain recipes more difficult(subsequent discussions with other scholars have pointed to larger fruit with a higher water content as being the culprit). The blogging component was also useful for learning about how to draw in readers with this format.

As someone who had become accustomed to writing for an academic audience, my shift to the blogging world (which began a year earlier with my library research blog) was an opportunity to learn how to effectively write in different contexts. For example, I would provide hyperlinks to websites throughout the blog text, but many of these would not be the same types of sources I would use in a scholarly paper. In one instance, the best comparison of several eastern European cookies came from About.com, and so I linked to that. Using less research-oriented resources was a good way to give the blog appeal to those outside of academia, and a great way to provide concise and clear definitions and examples that the casual reader wouldn't have to search an article for. I also based my citation decisions on what was available on the open web: many scholarly resources are housed in subscription-only databases that most readers of food blogs would not have access to. If I shared those sources, I would make it so most readers could not follow all the sources I used, and might risk limiting my readership. As Open Access publishing becomes more widely accepted, my future work in this area might be able to point to scholarly and popular resources equally.

The project also taught me that interacting with readers on a food blog was different than interacting with readers on my more general professional blog. This could be because, in that case, I had more time to build up readership and connect with others on Twitter and Facebook, which had resulted in a steadily-increasing readership. With the Modernizing Markham blog, I had few Twitter followers and only one subscriber, making it harder for my writing to have the reach it otherwise might. I did keep a close eye on the analytics (or statistics concerning traffic on the site), which helped me understand what readers may be looking for in a small-scale digital humanities site like mine.

The number of visitors to the site fluctuated dramatically over the course of the project. June through September 2010 saw less than ten readers a month before the project picked up steam and brought in 158 readers in October. From November to March, site views fluctuated between 100 and 250 views per month. The months with the highest views were those in which recipes along with historical information or suggested further readings were published, suggesting that readers saw the blog as a source for information beyond what they might find on other recipe blogs. Many visitors were referred from search engines, with approximately fifty different queries guiding readers to the site over the course of the project. The most frequently used queries were those related to cooking techniques contemporary to Markham (e.g. "wet suckets" or "quince marmalade") which suggested to me that there is an interest in learning about and preparing historic foods. Many other queries focused on information about Markham (both about his works in general and *The English Housewife* specifically), which also indicated that demand exists for writings that address his work.

Readers were also referred from links to my blog elsewhere on the web. One was my *Indiana Food Review* interview about the project in January 2011. The other was an article in *The Guardian* on how to cook the perfect pancake (Ireland, 2011; Cloake, 2011). The second article included a discussion of the pancake through history and linked to my blog when Markham was referenced. Readers also clicked on many of the hyperlinks I included in my text. Some of the most-used hyperlinks were those providing historical information about different foods (several from the site historicfood.com), although the link to the krumkake (wafer) iron I purchased and the link to the *Indiana Food Review* article were the most frequently visited.

The number of page views was also an important indicator of readership, because it showed which posts and pages readers found most interesting . The home page was the most-viewed page by a very large margin, which was a mistake on my part that makes the statistics harder to interpret (rather than adding page breaks in posts, I made new posts visible from the homepage, which meant readers did not have to click the post itself to read it). Several recipes (wet suckets, wafers, and quince marmalade) were among the most-read pages, as were the "About the Project" and "About Markham" pages. The recipes that were most widely read were often retrieved in search results, so the user would go directly to the post rather than accessing it from the home page. My other posts that provided historical context (e.g. "Class and the English Housewife") or suggested further readings were well-read when they were first published, but received less views overall.

Readers were not as open to commenting on the blog as I initially hoped, although several posts did have strings of comments as readers offered suggestions or shared their experiences. I opened up a discussion about this on my library research blog later on, and learned that at least one reader and regular food blogger experienced the same problem. She indicated her lack of commentary on my blog was mostly due to a lack of time, and to not wanting to reiterate what had been said in previous comments. I tried an experiment by listing the blog in the Kindle store to see if that would encourage new readers or more commentary, but only ended up with a handful of subscribers.

The experience of blogging and using social media did give me the chance to learn new approaches that I can implement in future projects. First of all, I was not as diligent in using social media as I should have been. I updated the Twitter account when I made a new post, but did not use it all that often to retweet relevant information shared by the users I followed on Twitter. I also did not actively follow other users on Twitter, and would want to devote more time to finding and following scholars, food bloggers, and cultural institutions. I would also make a Facebook page, which would give readers another way to connect with my work and a way to comment on posts that may feel more comfortable to them.

These and other techniques may bring more traffic and discussion to the blog itself. On the Wordpress site, I would want to continue posting a mixture of historical research and recipes, as this seemed to generate the most interest. I would also ask more questions in social media and blog posts to generate discussion amongst readers. During this project, I did not share the URL on listservs (or e-mail lists with member-submitted content relating to a specific topic, such as book arts), but I may do this for my future work. I will also add page breaks to each post so that the number of page views are more precise and do not just cluster around the home page. The blog had a relatively large readership for being maintained by only one individual, but I hope to at least double that in future Markham projects. Although this initial project reached fewer readers than I hoped, it was a valuable learning experience and an enjoyable way to bring a piece of history back to life.

Class and 'The English Housewife'

These following are two brief essays I wrote as blog posts to help readers understand class and gender issues in early modern England. The first talked about the relationship between class and food, and the second discussed cookery manuals during this time, as well as the woman's role in the home and women's literacy during this period. The tone of these posts, as well as most other posts on the blog, is more informal than most academic writing. This was done in the hopes of making academic research appealing to people who may not be accustomed to interacting with materials written in a formal, scholarly tone.

Foodstuffs and Class in
The English Housewife

During the project, I spent a lot of time talking about *The English Housewife* as an instruction manual and as a place to learn about cookery. What I spent less time with was the issue of class and audience: issues that would give us a better picture of who the English Housewife actually was. Beyond her gender and marital status, the title doesn't tell us much, but we do know enough about Markham to make some pretty good guesses. Markham is particularly interesting to me because he is writing for a country audience (this and his other books focus on activities that would be undertaken by a husbandman, or small landowner, and his wife), and because he encourages frugality (later authors seem a bit more lavish).

In order to start thinking about class and cookery manuals, it's important to know what the different classes were eating. Social classes were different from how we think of them today–rather than having a 'middle class' there were 'middling sorts,' which is kind of a hodgepodge term (that I still have trouble defining well) for those who lived comfortably but were not gentlemen/noblemen. The 'gentry' were gentleman landowners, whose social status would have been a bit higher. When I wrote about Markham's banqueting menu, one thing readers noticed was that the menu was mostly vegetarian. That's not to say that vegetarianism was a common concept in the 17th century (in fact, vegetarian monastic orders were heavily criticized by authors of books on health, who felt a lack of meat shortened one's life: see Albala 201-202), but rather that there seems to be a misconception that only meat, and not much else, was eaten during this time.

Markham does include another menu for a feast that includes a large number of meat dishes, but both this and the banqueting menu I worked from are noted as not being "of regular use," although they are still important for the housewife to be able to cook on special occasions (Best, 110). Meat had fallen in price in the time after the Black Plague, but its cost had risen by Markham's time when meat would have been available regularly only to the elite. Most people ate meat less frequently than the rich or ate less expensive cuts, like organ meat (Albala, 188). Vegetables made up the majority of the diet of the lower classes, who could not afford to have meat or dairy regularly. Meat was commonly eaten by the nobility in the middle ages, but plant-based foods became more popular and began their ascent up the social ladder during this time (Thirsk, 4-8).

Cookery and household manuals like Markham's helped to ensure the place of fruits and vegetables on middling tables. These books taught proper social graces and the newest food preparations, and so their inclusion of vegetables made those foods seem fashionable (Schoonover, 20-21). The food on one's table was indicative of social standing, but was also seen almost as a determinant of status: a peasant eating the food of the peasantry would absorb those elements within the food making it crude, while a courtier's consumption of exquisite foods served not only as a symbol of wealth, sophistication, and power but also as that courtier's embodiment of those qualities (Albala, 184).

Cookery Manuals and Class

Most cookery manuals during this time were directed toward middling sorts and gentry, and enjoyed increasing popularity along with other self-help and how-to manuals (Cormack and Massio, 79-84). Other manuals, such as John Murrell's *A Daily Exercise for Ladies and Gentlewomen* were more likely to focus on providing readers with the newest ways to prepare popular dishes. Markham's approach was unique because he offered some of these preparations, but did so more to provide a well-rounded background in homemaking to his readers, who would need to prepare such dishes for special occasions (see Best, 110). He emphasized thrift, and encouraged the use of items grown in the kitchen garden or otherwise available in the home. This may have been due in part to his own social status; Markham was a gentleman who saw his family's wealth and status decline over the course of his life. If you would like a more complete biography of Markham, make sure to read Best's introduction.

The women who read Markham's book would have been educated enough to be literate, but were also of a social standing where they were still directly involved within household tasks. Middling women (whose husbands owned estates or ran businesses) worked alongside servants to assist with the growing and preparation of food, and the production of household goods (Mendelson and Crawford, 307). While women in the gentry and merchant classes also supervised workers and organized household affairs, they were much more directly involved in household labor than noblewomen, who directed the labors of large numbers of servants without direct involvement in those tasks (Mendelson and Crawford, 307-309). Middling women also were likely to be literate: David Cressy placed the gentry along with the clergy and professionals on the "accomplished end of the literacy scale," and his research showed at least a thirty percentage point difference between them and the next most literate group, comprised of yeomen and tradesmen (Cressy, 124).

Joan Thirsk suggested that Markham's writing bridged the gap between the gentry and laboring classes through his simple recipes and his focus on economy (Thirsk, 91-92). While his work may have been more accessible to the laboring classes, his use of spices and other imported ingredients situated it solidly within the body of work aimed at a gentry/middling audience. Early modern literacy rates show that *The English Housewife* would have been inaccessible to most members of the lower classes (including the housewife's servants). Literacy among servants in most of England was low, akin to husbandmen and laborers, with an estimated seventy-six percent of servants being illiterate. Only servants in London were more likely to be literate, with a surprisingly low thirty-one percent illiteracy rate (Cressy, 129). These low literacy rates provide some insight into how the book was used: a number of the book's sections guided the reader in overseeing tasks that required multiple servants to complete (such as serving a feast). Since the servants were probably illiterate, this bolsters the claim that the book was used by the housewives themselves as they directly supervised their servants' work.

The Markham Meal

During the course of the project, my committee suggested that I select dishes to build a "Markham meal" rather than modernizing a hodgepodge of recipes. I turned to the text of *The English House-wife* to learn what items Markham would include in a menu, and since he did not have menus for everyday fare, I looked to his feasting and banqueting sections. Markham's "Ordering of banquets" (Best, pg 121) illustrated the variety of foods eaten at this sort of meal:

> "I will now proceed to the ordering or setting forth of a banquet; where in you shall observe that marchpanes have the first place, the middle place, and last place; your preserved fruits

shall be dished up first, your pastes next, your wet suckets after them, then your dried suckets, then your marmalades and goodinyakes, then your comfits of all kinds; next, your pears, apples, wardens baked, raw or roasted, and your oranges and lemons sliced, and lastly your wafer cakes. Thus you shall order them in the closet; but when they go to the table, you shall first send forth a dish made for show only, as beast, bird, fish, or fowl, according to invention: then your marchpane, then preserved fruit, then a paste, then a wet sucket, then a dry sucket, marmalade, comfits, apples, pears, wardens, oranges, and lemons sliced; and then wafers, and another dish of preserved fruits, and so consequently all the rest before: no two dishes of one kind going or standing together, and this will not only appear delicate to the eye, but invite the appetite with the much variety thereof."

I created a list of the different courses, organized by the order in which they were carried to the table. I consolidated

some of his recipes for candies and preserved fruit to avoid repetition and make
the project more manageable. I came up
with the following:

1. *Beast/Bird/Fish/Fowl for show:*
   This would have usually been a
   very elegant and expensive dish,
   but based on what was available
   in Iowa, I chose one of his chicken
   dishes.

2. *Marchpane (marzipan):* Traditionally this would have been baked
   onto a wafer and topped with different shaped pieces of marzipan
   and perhaps some gilding. I was
   not skilled enough to make marzipan shapes, although I did still
   make the marzipan wafers.

3. *Preserved fruit:* The way this was
   worded in the banqueting menu
   made it unclear whether Markham
   meant preserved whole fruits or
   fruit preserves (such as jam). After
   some consideration, I combined
   this category with the marmalade
   (which appears later on in his list)
   to create his recipes for white and
   red quince marmalade.

4. *Paste:* A paste of fruit and sugar

that's been baked. This was the recipe that resulted in several failed attempts before I gave up, although I understand that it may have been successful to use something with a very high pectin content (like quince).

5. *Candies:* Markham listed wet suckets (candied fruit in syrup), along with dry suckets and comfits (more like today's hard candies). I created the wet suckets using orange peel, and discovered that if I laid them out on wax paper, they hardened into a close approximation of what I understood a dry sucket to be like.

6. *Apples, pears, wardens (cooking pears):* These were baked, raw, or roasted, and so I chose to make a pie using cooking apples.

7. *Wafers:* These were very thin, sweet cookies, served as a digestive at the end of a meal. The batter was filled with cinnamon and rosewater.

I chose this menu over the much larger feast menu because of its affordability and the fact that it was more feasible for one person relying on a small apartment kitchen. The other menu Markham included laid out what would be included in a great feast and in a more humble feast. This menu included several pages of vegetable dishes, broths, and at least a dozen roasted or boiled meat dishes. Even the 'humble feast' still included 32 dishes (Best, 121-124). Both the feasting menus and the banquet menu were in Markham's section on 'conceited dishes,' which meant that they would have been reserved for special occasions when it was necessary to impress guests. Many of Markham's other recipes (such as oats and pancakes) would have been consumed as a part of everyday meals.

Recipes

Boiled Chicken

This recipe was the only meat dish included in the banquetting menu. Although chicken may not have traditionally been the meat chosen for a dish used for show, Markham offered a very appealing recipe for it (Best, 79):

"If you will boil chickens, young turkeys, peahens, or any house fowl daintily, you shall, after you have trimmed them, drawn them, trussed them, and washed them, fill their bellies as full of parsley as they can hold; then boil them with salt and water only till they be enough: then take a dish and put into it verjuice, and butter, and salt, and when the butter is melted, take the parsley out of the chickens' bellies, and mince it very small, and put it into the ver-juice and butter, and stir it well together; then lay in the chickens, and trim the dish with sippets, and so serve it forth."

This recipe was one of the few chicken recipes in *The English Housewife* (a much more accessible option for modern readers than capon, or rooster.) Most recipes dealt with fish/seafood, lamb, and waterfowl, with the occasional mention of capon and pork. The most common preparations laid out directions for boiling the meat or roasting it on a spit. Verjuice (from red grapes) was popular on both poultry and darker meats. This recipe, like many of the meat recipes, was very simple: most involved flavoring/stuffing the meat and then placing it in boiling water or on a spit before plating with a sauce.

One note about the modernized recipe: I used a small chicken, so adjust as times and measurements as necessary based on the size of your bird.

Boiled Chicken

- 1 whole chicken
- kitchen twine, for trussing
- Sea salt
- 1 cup light-bodied, tannic red wine (a Cabernet Sauvignon would be good here)
- 2 tbsp butter
- 1 bunch parsley

1. In a large stockpot, bring to a boil enough water to cover the chicken and some salt.
2. Take the bunch of parsley and cut of the stems.
3. Holding the bunch tightly, push it into the chicken cavity as far as it will go (leaving too much stem sticking out will make it more difficult to truss the chicken).
4. Truss the chicken.
5. Place the chicken into the boiling water and cook until the chicken is done (it springs back when touched and the juice runs clear). Set aside until it is cooled just enough to retrieve the parsley stuffing.
6. In a saucepan, bring the wine to a simmer with 1/2 tsp salt. Add the butter and continue gently simmering.

7. Meanwhile, chop the parsley finely and add to the sauce.
8. Pour the sauce over the chicken in a serving dish.

Markham's boiled chicken recipe, 1631 edition.

Marzipan

Marchpane (marzipan) appeared as an accompaniment to many dishes in Markham's time, and is mentioned in his banquetting menus. Marchpane was a flat disk of almond paste decorated with other sweets (Bell, 2011). In Markham's day, the paste would have been created using a mortar and pestle, but I altered the recipe a bit to account for a food processor or blender. One side effect of this alteration is that my marzipan had a more coarse texture than most marzipans, so to get a finer-textured and more authentic marzipan, make sure to use a mortar and pestle (a stone mortar and pestle can often be found at Asian grocery stores, and are usually inexpensive).

Here's Markham's original recipe (Best, 116):

> "To make the best marchpane, take the best Jordan almonds and blanch them in warm water, then put them into a stone mortar, and with a wooden pestle beat them to a pap, then take of the finest refined sugar well searced, and with it, and damask rose-water, beat it to a good stiff paste, allowing almost to every Jordan almond three spoonful of sugar; then when it is brought thus to a paste, lay it upon a fair table, and, strewing searced sugar under it, mould it like leaven; then with a rolling pin roll it forth, and lay it upon wafers washed with rose-water; then pinch it about the sides, and put it into what form you please; then strew searced sugar all over it; which done, wash it over with rose-water and sugar mixed together, for that will make the ice; then adorn it with comfits, gilding, or whatsoever devices you please, and

so set it into a hot stove, and there back it crispy, and so serve it forth. Some use to mix with the paste cinnamon and ginger finely searced, but I refer that to your particular taste."

Michael Best's endnotes provided some helpful insight on the proportions Markham described. For the proportion of sugar to almonds, Markham suggested 3 spoonfuls of sugar per almond, but Best found that other authors suggested a 2:1 ratio of sugar to almonds, which I initially chose because it was easier to remember. I used slivered, blanched almonds to avoid ruining my food processor, so after several attempts I found that the ratio needed to be altered to account for this.

After testing the recipe, it became evident that, with granulated sugar, only a 1:1 ratio of sugar to almonds is needed before it started getting too crumbly. That made it a little harder to work with, but the results were mostly successful. The largest problem I had with this recipe was in shaping the marzipan into decorative shapes. Several times, I tried to press the marzipan directly on to the wafer cookie, but that caused the wafer to crack. One solution for this is to press the marzipan into a decorative pan or mold and shape it that way. It's important to note that the recipe requires wafers to put the paste on before baking, so make sure to prepare some beforehand.

Marzipan

- 1/2 c. blanched, slivered almonds
- 1/2 c. granulated sugar, plus extra for dusting
- 1 tbsp rosewater, plus extra for topping

1. Place almonds in food processor and pulse until finely chopped. Add rosewater, pulse once or twice, then add the sugar (if it's too crumbly, try adding a tiny bit more rosewater.)
2. Turn the mixture out onto a cutting board or counter dusted with sugar, and roll or pat out.
3. Place the mixture on a wafer cookie that's been lightly brushed with rosewater, being careful not to break the cookie (it helps to put the cookie on the baking sheet beforehand to avoid transferring it. You can also press the marzipan into a mold before placing it on the cookies).

4. Brush marzipan with rosewater, then sprinkle with sugar.
5. Place in a 500 degree oven and bake for about 5 minutes (long enough to harden the marzipan a bit, but not enough to burn the cookies or melt the sugar).

Wafers

Wafers are a very thin cookie, originally developed as a digestive aid for the end of wealthy feasts (Day, 2003). I did not find a modern equivalent of the exact recipe, although similar wafer cookies with different flavorings have come from Eastern European and Nordic traditions (Rolek, 2011). The largest drawback for wafer making by the modern cook is the fact that wafer irons are not a common household appliance. After researching on a number of sites, I found a cast iron model that was more reasonably priced than others available online, and was a stovetop model rather than an electric iron or one requiring an open fire, which made it easier to use. (Danish windmill, 2011.) It was technically a Nordic Krumkake pan, but was the most affordable solution: antique wafer irons that were closer to those used by women in Markham's time could cost hundreds of dollars (and possibly more). These were similar to modern krumkake irons, but had a long wooden and metal handle for holding them near the fire to cook. Pizelle irons and other wafer irons are available as well, although many of these are electric models. A wafer iron can be used to prepare any kind of wafer cookie, although I have not yet discovered a flavor combination I enjoy as much as the rosewater and cinnamon that Markham used (Best, 117):

> "To make the best wafers, take the finest wheat flour you can get, and mix it with cream, the yolks of eggs, rose-water, sugar, and cinnamon til it be a little thicker than pancake batter; and then, warming your wafer irons on a charcoal fire, anoint them first with sweet butter, and then lay your batter and press it, and bake it white or brown at your pleasure."

My recipe yields about fifteen cookies. Make sure to preheat your iron on medium-low heat for a few minutes before adding any batter.

Wafer cookies

-1 cup flour
-1/2 cup sugar
-1 tsp ground cinnamon
-3 egg yolks
-1/4 cup rosewater (available in Middle Eastern markets or Asian food stores)
-1 cup cream

1. Combine all ingredients in a bowl and whisk until smooth.
2. Grease your iron with a little butter, and add one rounded tablespoon of batter to the center.
3. Close the iron and hold closed tightly for about 30 seconds to press the pattern on the iron into the cake.
4. Continue cooking for about 2 minutes or until golden brown, turning the iron over once to ensure both sides are cooked.
5. Allow to cool on a plate or rack before transferring the cooled wafers to anoth-

er plate (this keeps them from getting soggy).

Wet Suckets (Candied Orange Peels)

"Wet sucket" is one of the more unappetizing culinary terms I've run across, but Markham and his contemporaries would have understood it as referring to fruit in syrup. Wet suckets appeared in England in the early 17th century (Davidson and Jaine, 2006), right around the time Markham was compiling *The English Housewife*. They were made using fruit, vegetables, roots (like Angelica root), and nuts. Markham's recipe is as follows (Best, 120):

> "Take curds, the parings of lemons, of oranges or pomecitrons, or indeed any half ripe green fruit, and

boil them till they be tender, in sweet wort; then make a syrup in this sort: take three pound of sugar, and the whites of four eggs, and a gallon of water; then swinge and beat the water and the eggs together, and then put in your sugar, and set it on the fire, and let it have an easy fire, and so let it boil six or seven walms, and then strain it through a cloth, and let it seethe again till it fall from the spoon, and then put it into the rinds of fruits."

There are a number of terms worth explaining from this recipe: wort (or sweet wort) is "the liquor made by an infusion of malt in water, from which beer and ale are fermented" (Best, 312). I have never brewed beer, but from what I understand from my brewing friends, wort is the substance one has prior to adding the hops. I did not have access to wort or malt, so I used the closest (and admittedly not entirely similar) flavoring I had on hand: malt whiskey. The flavor was very good (whiskey and orange complement each other well), although if you know a brewer you may want to ask them to set aside a bit of wort for you. A few other terms in the recipe: pomecitron (a member of the citrus family), swinge (to whip or beat), and walm (to boil).

There were a few things I learned when testing this recipe. First, don't whisk the mixture too vigorously or you'll end up with meringue on top. Markham suggested straining the mixture (I found that I had a few bits of egg in mine that I fished out with a spoon), so do not worry if you have some bits of cooked egg in your mixture. When you're finished, you will have a very thick syrup (egg white has been widely used as a thickener in foods and as a binder in all sorts of other things, including photographs). Add your fruit, toss to coat, and put it in a jar. I had quite a bit of syrup (more than I needed for the oranges), so I also prepared some wet suckets using ginger. Also, the sugar will crystallize a bit after it has been sitting out for a few hours (although it will never make the candies hard all the way through). If you would like to have a slight sugar crust on the fruit, spread it on a wax paper-lined cookie sheet.

Wet Suckets

For the peels:
-4 oranges
-1/4 whiskey
-2 c. water

1. Using a vegetable peeler, peel strips of orange rind, being careful to not get too much of the bitter white pith. Cut into bite sized pieces (1/4"-1/2" long).
2. Boil the whiskey and water in a saucepan and add the orange peels. Boil until tender (about 10 to 15 minutes). (Side note: When I prepared the ginger, I peeled it with the back of a spoon, sliced it, then cut the slices into thin strips).
3. Drain.

For the syrup:
-2 egg whites
-8 cups water (make sure its cold or room temperature)
-3 1/2 cups sugar

1. Whisk egg whites into water until incorporated.
2. Heat slowly over medium-low heat, stirring frequently to ensure that the egg

doesn't scramble. While heating, add the sugar to the water, 1/2 cup at a time.

3. Boil for 30-45 minutes, or until the syrup is very thick (for those who have made caramel, you want it to coat a spoon in the way caramel sauce does).

4. Let cool slightly, then toss the orange peels into the syrup and pour the mixture into a jar.

To speake then of the mixture and kneading of pasts, *Of the mixture of pasts.* you shall vnderstand that your rye paste would be kneaded onely with hot water and a little butter, or sweete seame and Rye flower very finely sifted, and it would be made tough & stiffe, that it may stand well in the rising, for the coffin therof must euer be very deepe; your course wheat crust would be kneaded with hot water, or Mutton broth, and good store of butter, and the paste made stiffe and tough, becaufe that coffin must be deepe alfo; your fine wheat crust must be kneaded with as much butter as water, and the past made reafonable ly the and gentle, into which you muft put three or foure egges or more, according to the quantity you blend together, for they will giue it a fufficient ftiffening.

Markham's directions for making pastry, 1631 edition.

Pippin Pie

Markham had a number of recipes for pie in The English Housewife, but "pippin pie" looked the most appealing to me. Pippins are cooking apples, and his pie recipe was very similar to his recipe for "codling tart" except that the pippin pie included dates and oranges. Over the centuries, both sweet and savory pies were used as a method of preservation (Food Timeline, 2000). In modern pie crusts, cold fat is cut into the flour, but pie crusts in Markham's time were made much differently: the fat was cooked with water, and the hot mixture was added to the flour to form the dough. The crust from this time was called a coffin, and it was filled either with sweet fillings or savory fillings (mostly meat).

There are a number of good resources online with information about coffins in the Middle Ages. Medieval Cookery (2010) provides a good breakdown of different recipes for crusts. Although it references materials made before *The English Housewife*, understanding how pies were made in the previous centuries helped me understand how they evolved. The best discussion of coffins I found online was from Monica Gaudio (2009). Gaudio's recipes were particularly useful because she showed a 14th century pie recipe and a 16th century pie recipe, with some discussion of how the two recipes differ and the historical context of each.

Harold McGee also talked a bit about these pastries in his book, *On Food and Cooking*. He traced the roots of hot-water pastry to the Middle Ages, where it served as a container for meat dishes needing to be preserved for some time. The crust itself was tender to eat, but sturdy enough to retain cooking juices. It was made with a large amount of water (fifty parts water per one hundred parts flour, along with thirty-five parts lard). The water and fat were heated to almost boiling, and the flour was stirred in just until it formed a mass, then the dough was rested. The large amount of fat limited gluten development which helped make the crust tender, and repelled water, which kept cooking juices from breaking down the pastry. (McGee, 568). Markham's pie required two recipes: one for the dough (Best, 96-98) and one for the filling (Best, 104):

"On the Mixture of Pastes:
To speak then of the mixture and kneading of pastes, you shall understand that your rye paste be kneaded only with hot water and a little butter, or sweet seam and rye flour very finely sifted, and it would be made tough and stiff that it may stand well in the raising, for the coffin thereof must ever be very deep; your coarse wheat crust would be kneaded with hot water, or mutton broth and a good store of butter, and the paste made stiff and deep because that coffin must be deep also; your fine wheat crust must be kneaded with as much butter as water, and the paste made reasonable lithe and gentle, into which

you must put three or four eggs or more according to the quantity you blend together, for they will give it a sufficient stiffening."

"A Pippin Pie
Take the fairest and best pippins, and pare them, and make a hole in the top of them; then prick in each hole a clove or two, then put them into the coffin, then break in whole sticks of cinnamon and slices of orange peels and dates, and on the top of every pippin a little piece of sweet butter: then fill the coffin, and cover the pippins over with sugar; then close up the pie, and bake it, as you bake pies of the like nature, and when it is baked anoint the lid over with store of sweet butter, and then strew sugar upon it a good thickness, and set it into the oven again for a little space, as whilst the meat is in dishing up, and then serve it."

I chose the fine wheat crust, which differed from Gaudio's recipe in that it included eggs. Gretchen Miller (n.d.) provided a modernized version of the coffin recipe and gave me permission to reproduce it here. For the filling, I followed Markham's suggestions and kept the apples whole. I used small Ginger Gold apples I found at the farmer's market, peeled them, and cored them by using a paring knife to cut a circle around the top. I arranged them in the crust, putting cloves inside each one. Then, I pitted the dates and arranged them around the apples so everything stayed in place. I placed orange peels and whole cinnamon sticks between the apples to flavor the pie (for those in a household with children, replace the whole spices with ground ones). Markham instructed readers to put pats of butter on each apple and sprinkle them with sugar before putting on the top crust, so I also did this. After it baked for a while, the crust was brushed with melted butter and sprinkled with sugar (I used turbinado sugar, which is less processed and closer to what was used historically). I used a 9-inch cake pan rather than creating the thicker coffin with freestanding sides.

Pippin pie

For the crust:
- -1/4 cup plus 2 tbsp water
- -1 stick butter
- -2 1/2 cups flour
- -3 egg yolks

For the filling:
- -8 small cooking apples, peeled
- -16 whole cloves
- -The peels of two oranges
- -4 cinnamon sticks, halved
- -12 dates
- -Butter
- -1/2 cup sugar, plus more for dusting

1. Preheat oven to 350.
2. Combine water and butter in a pan and simmer until butter melts.
3. Meanwhile, stir egg yolks into the flour until evenly mixed.
4. Make a well in the center of the flour mixture, and pour the butter mixture in. Stir to combine, then knead until it forms a dough ball.
5. Divide the ball in half, and roll out into two circles a bit larger than your pan (I made two crusts each with a diameter

of roughly eleven inches).

6. Grease the bottom and sides of a 9" round pan, and put the bottom crust in, making sure it also covers the sides of the pan.

7. Using a paring knife, cut a hole in the top of each apple and remove the seeds, and put two cloves in each apple. Arrange in the crust.

8. Arrange the dates in the open spaces around the apples, then evenly distribute the orange peels and cinnamon sticks.

9. Place a small pat of butter on top of each apple, and sprinkle the entire filling with 1/2 cup sugar.

10. Roll out the top crust, and place on top of the pie.

11. Bake at 350 for 75 minutes, or until the apples are tender and the crust is just golden brown.

12. Brush the crust with melted butter and sprinkle with sugar, then continue baking for 10-15 minutes.

Quince Marmalade

In some parts of the U.S., quince fruit is in season in Autumn and can be found in some grocery stores. In northern states (including Iowa, where I lived), it is harder to find and sometimes must be ordered online. I used Diamond Organics (2010), although they remove the listing from their site when it is not in season. Since shipping for perishables can be expensive, this simple recipe is a good way to experiment with preparing quince with a very low risk of failure.

Quince was one of the most popular fruits in Markham's day–it appeared probably more often than any other fruit in *The English Housewife*, and the same trend can be found in other books from this time. The history of the quince as an ingredient goes back to ancient times, and although they aren't especially common now in the U.S., they are a popular addition to recipes elsewhere in the world. The fruit is especially useful in preserves because of its high pectin content (Damrosch, 2008), which serves as a thickener.

The English Housewife included recipes for red quince marmalade and white quince marmalade (Best, 112):

"Marmalade of Quinces Red
To make red marmalade of quinces; take a pound of quinces and cut them in halves, and take out the cores and pare them; then take a pound of sugar and a quart of fair water and put them all into a pan, and let them boil with a soft fire, and sometimes turn them and keep them covered with a pewter dish, so that the steam or air may come a little out; the longer they are in boiling the better colour they will have; and when they be soft take a knife and cut them cross upon the top, it will make the syrup go through that they may be all of a like colour;

then set a little of your syrup to cool, and when it beginneth to be thick then break your quinces with a slice or a spoon, so small as you can in the pan, and then strew a little fine sugar in your box's bottom, and so put it up."

"Marmalade white
To make white marmalade you must in all points use your quinces as is beforesaid; only you must take but a pint of water to a pound of quinces, and a pound of sugar, and boil them as fast as you can, and cover them not at all."

I followed Markham's recipes and discovered that both are practically foolproof, especially for those who have made preserves in the past. There were a few useful tips I discovered while testing these recipes: First, in order to use as much fruit as possible, I peeled the fruit with a vegetable peeler rather than a knife. For the red marmalade, I gently boiled the fruit for as long as possible to fully develop its red color. The only difference in preparing the white marmalade was that I cooked it quickly to prevent it from changing color. Raw quince has a light, cream-colored flesh that will only change when cooked for extended periods (Emerson, 2005).

Red quince marmalade
-1 lb quince(s)
-2 1/4 c sugar
-4 c water

1. Peel the quince using a knife or vegetable peeler, cut it in half and remove the core.
2. Place in a medium saucepan with the water and sugar.
3. Simmer over a low heat, loosely covered, for about 2 hours. Turn fruit occasionally during cooking.
4. After the first half an hour, take a knife and made two perpendicular cuts on the outside of each half.
5. Once most of the water has evaporated and the fruit is in a thick syrup, use a spoon or potato masher to break the quince apart into evenly distributed bits.
6. Allow to cool.

White quince marmalade

-1 lb. quince
-2 cups water
-2 1/4 cups sugar

1. Peel, halve, and core the quince.
2. Combine the halved fruit in a pot with the water and sugar.
3. Boil rapidly until a thick syrup develops (about 30 minutes), then break down the fruit with a spoon or potato masher to desired smoothness.

Strawberry Conserve

This project began with one of the simplest recipes from the book. Preservation was important for storing food without refrigeration, but this method was also considered healthful in Markham's time, because the fruit was cooked prior to being consumed (raw fruits and vegetables were seen as non-nutritious at best and poisonous at worst. For a more thorough discussion of this, see Albala, 2002). Markham's book was filled with recipes for preserves, in part because he urged readers to be frugal by growing and preparing as much of their own food as possible, and because it was necessary to store food in the winter months when fresh fruits and vegetables were not available. Preserved foods were a part of all early modern English cookery manuals, although I have yet to encounter one with as large a section on the subject as *The English Housewife*. I used the recipe called "to make any conserve" (Best, 116).

> "To make conserve of any fruit you please, you shall take the fruit you intend to make conserve of; and if it be stone fruit you shall take out the stones; if other fruit, take away the paring and core, and then boil them in fair running water to a reasonable height; then drain them from thence, and put them into a fresh vessel with claret wine, or white wine, according to the colour of the fruit: and so boil them to a thick pap all to mashing, breaking, and stirring them together; then to every pound of pap put to a pound of sugar, and so stir them all well together, and, being very hot, strain them through fair strainers, and so pot it up."

The modern jam recipe I used the past called for the ingredients to be boiled and reduced down to the finished product, rather than strained. I had looked at several different jam recipes from Markham's time period, and the method described above was fairly typical. The fruit itself was also different from what would be used today. Modern strawberry hybrids come from species native to the Americas (Encyclopedia Britannica, 2011), but other strawberries were available in Europe at this time too. The species was called 'fraises de bois' (literally 'strawberries of wood' or wild strawberries), and was found around western Europe (Ken Albala, personal communication, October 12, 2010).

For centuries, the only strawberries available in Europe were wild varieties that grew at the edges of wooded areas, and were known by a variety of names. The term "strawberry" came from the English practice of placing straw under the fruits to keep the off the damp soil. They were not cultivated until the 15th century, in part because of the amount of room they took up and because they drained the soil of nutrients so had to be rotated occasionally (Toussaint-Samat, 652). The more tart fruits were usually used for jams(Ken Albala, personal communication, October 12, 2010), a practice seen throughout Markham's book. Quinces were also very popular for preserves, as were oranges. Markham also had a recipe for a "conserve of flowers" (Best, 117).

This recipe and the others of its time were not written using the measurements we use today (cups, tablespoons, teaspoons, etc.). Early modern cookery manuals were more of a general guide rather than a specific set of instructions, so many of the recipes used weights (if they provided any specific measure at all) and guided the reader by describing how the food looked or felt during cooking, instead of using times and temperatures (cooking temperatures were not as exact as a thermometer in a modern oven, so these measures would have been less useful).

Strawberry conserve

-4 c strawberries, sliced
-water
-1/4 c Cabernet Sauvignon (or other
 light-bodied red wine)
-1/4 c sugar

1. In a medium saucepan, place the strawberries in the bottom and add enough water to cover them. Bring to boil, and cook until very soft (about 20 minutes).
2. Using a fine strainer, strain the liquid from the strawberries and add to a high-sided skillet. Add the wine, and bring to a boil.
3. While the mixture is boiling, use a potato masher to mash the fruit into a pulp.
4. Turn off the heat and add the sugar, stir until dissolved.
5. Using a fine strainer, strain excess liquid from the mixture and place into a heat-proof container.

Suggested Further Readings & Terminology

This section was compiled from several blog posts that I wrote in response to readers' requests for other sources about early modern cooking. I tried to include suggestions for information on historic recipes, additional resources for scholarly research, and clarifications of Early Modern terminology.

Cooking Resources for the Confused

When I engaged in conversation about this project, I noticed that many people felt timid about trying historic recipes because they felt uncomfortable with the techniques. In order to help people learn a bit more about historic cookery and become more comfortable with what the recipes entail, I compiled this list of resources:

Ken Albala and Rosanna Nafziger. The Lost Art of Real Cooking. New York: Penguin, 2010.

This book is incredibly useful, and is one that I turn to when trying a new technique more often than any other. It's a great way to learn more about food preparation done by hand, and helps get the reader into the mindset of cooking food the way it was done in the past. The authors' style is approachable and casual, and there are illustrations for some of the steps that you might not be familiar with (e.g. making a lattice pie crust). There is also background information about how the recipes were prepared historically (and how some of the ingredients or techniques have changed).

Gillian Riley, Renaissance Recipes. San Francisco: Pomegranate Artbooks, 1993.
This book is a good introduction to Renaissance Italian food. It includes recipes that are simple to prepare, along with paintings and historical background. I received it as a gift, and it's a beautiful book to look at and fun to cook from.

Maxine McKendry, Seven Hundred Years of English Cooking. Ed. By Arabella Boxer. New York: Exeter Books, 1983.
Nell Heaton, Traditional Recipes of the British Isles. London: Faber and Faber Limited, 1951.
I learned about both these books through David Schoonover's (ed.) Ladie

Borlase's Receiptes Booke (1998). For a project like *Modernizing Markham*, these books were useful because they allowed me to see how other authors had modernized recipes. Most of the recipes are not directly contemporary to Markham's time, but they are still a good resource for those wanting to learn about how food was prepared in the past.

Mollie Katzen, The New Enchanted Broccoli Forest. Berkeley: Ten Speed Press, 2000.

Mollie Katzen's books will always have a special place in my heart after receiving The New Enchanted Broccoli Forest as a birthday gift from one of my dearest friends. Beyond sentimental reasons, Katzen's book is unique because the entire thing is lettered and illustrated by her (and is a part of my inspiration for illustrating and lettering my modernized recipes from this project).

Harold McGee, On Food and Cooking: The Science and Lore of the Kitchen. Scribner: New York, 2004.

This is an excellent reference to have on hand, and it covers a very broad range of topics. McGee explains how different foods are made, the chemistry behind the technique or combination of ingredients that creates the finished product, and the history of the dish or ingredient.

Other Published Resources
on Gervase Markham

I have found quite a few good articles on Markham's *The English Housewife*, and discovered that since Markham's writing spanned so many disciplines, he invites study and criticism from a number of modern disciplines including history, medicine, and literary criticism. For those looking for more scholarly resources, or to approach the text from different perspectives, these resources are an excellent place to start. It should be noted that most of these articles do not focus exclusively on Markham, but they do situate his work, alongside other writings, within a larger discussion of a given topic.

Knoppers, Laura Lunger. "Opening the Queen's Closet: Henrietta Maria, Elizabeth Cromwell, and the Politics of Cookery." Renaissance Quarterly 60 (2007): 464-499.

This article examines the portrayal of powerful women in cookery manuals that were produced after Markham's. What struck me the most was the author's discussion of the Cromwells as the focal point of The Court & Kitchin of Elizabeth. The author notes that, while early manuals like Markham's applauded frugality and country living, this later book mocks that lifestyle (pg 487).

Leong, Elaine. "Making Medicines in the Early Modern Household." Bulletin of the History of Medicine 82, vol. 1 (2008) 145-168.

Markham is mentioned only briefly here, but the subject matter of this article reminds us of a very important part of The English Housewife that I did not explore. That is the matter of healthcare, which was a major part of the housewife's activities. Markham spent a lot of time talking about how to create and use treatments for a staggering array of ailments, many of which involved herbal compounds that were consumed or placed on the flesh. There was also a section on surgery, as minor procedures were considered a part of her duties.

Martin, Meredith. "Interiors and Interiority in the Ornamental Dairy Tradition." Eighteenth-Century Fiction 20, vol. 3, (2008): 357-384.
   This article deals with Markham's writing on dairies, found later in *The English Housewife*, in great depth. She uses Markham's work to discuss women's role in the English dairy. She also relates the attributes Markham encouraged in the housewife (purity, patience, gentleness, delicacy, and charity) to the ways other books classified "good" women (pgs 358-359). She also clarifies the role of servants in this setting: Markham's work was directed toward literate middling and upper-class women, but dairy work would have been done largely by female servants, with the housewife herself performing more of a supervisory function (pg 359).

Wall, Wendy. "Why Does Puck Sweep?: Fairylore, Merry Wives, and Social Struggle." Shakespeare Quarterly 52, vol. 1 (2001),

Wall provides an insightful look into gender in early modern England, and while I recommend reading the whole article, there are a couple notes from it that are particularly relevant to this project. First is her note on page 77, where she shows that the first English cookbook was addressed to elite male readers, but that subsequent books (including Markham's) addressed women directly. Her citations are also an excellent place to locate information about other Early Modenr cookery manuals.

Mylander, Jennifer. "Early Modern 'How-To' Books: Impractical Manuals and the Construction of Englishness in the Atlantic World." The Journal for Early Modern Cultural Studies 9, vol. 1 (2009) 123-146.

Mylander discusses how Markham's book and similar works circulated across the Atlantic to find their way into Colonial American homes. Both Markham and Nicholas Culpeper (who wrote somewhat later) promoted self-sufficiency, and both of their books were amongst those that were shipped to the Americas (and were considered indispensable to colonists of all classes, see page 124). While Mylander does discuss *The English Housewife* specifically, she does place it in the context of his larger body of work, particularly in showing how his writing promoted 'English-ness,' as well as how the agricultural practices in his other books did not fit with the new world.

While not directly related to English cookery, Markham wrote many other texts on horsemanship, soldiery, hunting, and agriculture; he even wrote some fiction earlier in his life. Those texts are referenced in a number of scholarly articles that may be of interest, including:

McMullin, B.J. "Early 'Secular' Press Figures." The Library: The Transactions of the Bibliographical Society 10, vol. 1, (2009): 57-65.
This article mentions '*A Way to Get Wealth*' and '*Cheap and Good Husbandry*,' two of Markham's books aimed toward a male audience.

Golz, David. "Diamonds, Maidens, Widow Dido, and Cock-a-diddle-dow." Comparative Drama 43, vol. 2, (2009): 167-196.

Mentions 'The Dumb Knight,' a work of fiction by Markham. There are also many other articles that talk about his fictional writing within the context of contemporary literature.

Kelly, Ann Cline. "Gulliver as Pet and Pet Owner: Conversations with Animals in Book 4." ELH 74, vol. 2 (2007): 323-349.
Landry, Donna. "The Bloody Shouldered Arabian and Early Modern English Culture." Criticism 46, vol. 1 (2004): 41-69.

Both these articles talk a bit about Markham's numerous horsemanship manuals.

Benson, Sean. "'If I do prove her haggard': Shakespeare's Application of Hawking Tropes to Marriage." Studies in Philology 103, vol. 2 (2006): 186-207.

This text mentions Markham's book, *Country Contentments*, especially its advice for falconers.

Mullett, Charles F. "Gervase Markham: Scientific Amateur." Isis 35, vol. 2 (1944) 106-118.

While this article is significantly older than the others, I like it because it gives an overview of Markham's different writings and their subject matter.

Wall, Wendy. "Renaissance National Husbandry: Gervase Markham and the Publication of England." The Sixteenth Century Journal 27, vol. 3 (1996) 767-785.
This article discusses Markham's writing as a whole, and focuses on his definitions of English agriculture as being distinct from that of other countries.

Suggestions for further reading on Early Modern Cookery

This list is as a reference for those looking to learn more about early modern English cookery, including many of the sources I have used in researching this project. I have tried to focus on sources that are accessible to those who may not have access to databases of early printed works: some of the original cookbooks I have looked at are not available in reprints (or at least not that I am aware of). It should be noted that these are all printed sources I accessed at the beginning of the project: other sources can be found in the 'Historical Background' section of the book, as well as the bibliography.

Albala, Ken. *Eating Right in the Renaissance*, University of California Press, 2002.

Albala, Ken. *Food in Early Modern Europe*, Greenwood Press, 2003

Albala, Ken, *Cooking in Europe: 1250-1650*, Greenwood Press, 2006

Albala, Ken, *The Banquet: Dining in the Great Courts of Late Renaissance Europe*, University of Illinois Press, 2007.

Albala, Ken. *"Cooking as Research Methodology: Experiments in Renaissance Cuisine"* in *Renaissance Food from Rabelais to Shakespeare: Culinary Readings and Culinary Histories*, Joan Fitzpatrick, ed. Ashgate Press, 2010.
Ken Albala has written on a number of subjects within food studies, and has a small body of work that focuses on Early Modern Europe that I found very useful in understanding the context in which The English Housewife was written.

Cormack, Bradin and Carla Mazzio. 2005. *Book Use, Book Theory: 1500-1700*. Chicago: University of Chicago Library.

Cormack and Mazzio's book is a wonderful introduction to book history, and is useful for those who are new to the subject aas well as those hoping to learn more about certain topics. It includes a section on self-help books and instruction manuals (under which cookery manuals can be classifed).

Cressy, David. 1980. Literacy and the Social Order: Reading and Writing in Tudor and Stuart England. Cambridge: Cambridge University Press.

Cressy's research is some of the clearest I've found on literacy in early modern England, and how patterns of literacy impacted social structure.

Markham, Gervase. The English Housewife. Edited by Michael Best. (1986). Canada: McGill-Queen's University Press.

This version of Markham's work is the most accessible for most readers, with paperback copies costing around $20. The introduction by Best provides a wonderful background in the subject, and the book includes the entirety of Markham's original work.

Mendelson, Sara and Crawford, Patricia. 1998. *Women in Early Modern England: 1550-1720*. Oxford: Oxford University Press.

Mendelson and Crawford discuss gender during this time period, providing a context for cookery texts in domestic life.

Schoonover, David E., ed. 1998. *Ladie Borlase's Receiptes Booke*. Iowa City: University of Iowa Press.

Schoonover's book is similar in layout to Best's. The introduction provides background information, and is followed by the original cookery manual text. Ladie Borlase's original book is held at the University of Iowa's Special Collections (in the Szathmary Culinary Collection, to be precise), and is a manuscript recipe book created by members of one household (rather than a text that was printed and purchased by members of many households, like Markham's).

Shammas, Carole. 1983. "Food Expenditures and Economic Well-Being in Early Modern England." *The Journal of Economic History*, 43(1)89-100.

Shammas explores the interplay between food and economics and the role both played in determining one's well-being and social status.

Spiller, Elizabeth. 2008. Seventeenth-century English recipe books: cooking, physic, chirurgery in the works of Elizabeth Talbot Grey and Aletheia Talbot Howard. Travitsky, Betty S. and Prescott, Anne Lake, ed. United Kingdom: Ashgate Publishing Ltd.

Spiller discusses the work of female cookery manual authors, and her findings are a useful point of comparison for my work and similar projects.

Thirsk, Joan. 2007. Food in Early Modern England: Phases, Fads, Fashions 1500-1760. London: Hambledon Continuum.

Thirsk provides a very thorough history of food during this time period, and does a wonderful job of tying food into the context of the larger culture.

Touissant-Samat, Maguelonne. 1992. History of Food. Trans: Anthea Bell. Malden, MA: Blackwell Publishing.

Touissant-Samat's book gives a great overview of how different foods have evolved over time. Especially useful are in-depth explorations of specific ingredients, in which the author discusses how these ingredients, and our use of them, has changed. It also includes very specific references to different practices of cultivation and methods of cooking.

Terminology for the Confused

A lot of the terms used in Markham and in the scholarly research surrounding cookery manuals may be unfamiliar to some readers, so I've created this section to offer a quick reference guide. Some of these definitions come from the incredibly useful glossary in Michael Best's edition of *The English Housewife*, and others I have learned from talking with food historians. I have restricted my this section to those that directly relate to the recipes I prepared for this project, so it is by no means an exhaustive list.

coffin: A pie crust. It was a very thick crust in the Middle Ages, and somewhat thinner by Markham's time.

comfit: Dried fruits, nuts, or spices that are covered in a candy coating.

dry sucket: Candied fruit or flowers.

middling sorts: This is the term used in scholarly research about this period to describe merchants and gentry, who were not at the top of the metaphorical social ladder (e.g. nobility), nor at the bottom (laborers). These groups had more prestige and wealth than laborers and peasants, but were less privileged than nobles.

pippin: Cooking apples.

quince: A fruit that is not as common today, but was popular in Markham's time. It grows on trees and is related to the pear. Its high pectin content makes it useful in preserves, and it changes color from white to red when cooked for long periods.

malt: sprouted grain used in brewing and distilling.

marchpane: Marzipan. It is a sweet almond paste that is still used today in desserts.

pomecitron: a member of the citrus family.

sallat: (cooked) salad.

strange: (as in "strange sallats"): "strange" usually referred to something that was foreign, so in cookery manuals this term is used to denote foreign dishes.

swinge: to whip or beat.

wafers: a very thin cookie, originally developed for the end of wealthy feasts to aid digestion.

walm: boil (in reference to boiling liquid).

wardens: cooking pears that keep well for long periods.

wet sucket: It sounds a little unappetizing, but it just refers to fruit in syrup.

Bibliography

Albala, Ken. *Eating Right in the Renaissance*. Berkeley: University of California Press, 2002.

Bell, Donald R. "Authentic Renaissance Marchpane Recipes." *Grandma's Homemade Dessert Recipes*, 2011 http://www.homemade-dessert-recipes.com/renaissance-marchpane-recipes.html

Cloake, Felicity. "How to Cook Perfect Pancakes." *The Guardian* (U.K.), Mar. 3, 2011. http://www.guardian.co.uk/lifeandstyle/wordofmouth/2011/mar/03/how-to-cook-perfect-pancakes

Cormack, Bradin and Carla Mazzio. 2005. *Book Use*, Book Theory: 1500-1700. Chicago: University of Chicago Library.

Cressy, David. 1980. *Literacy and the Social Order: Reading and Writing in Tudor and Stuart England.* Cambridge: Cambridge University Press.

Damrosch, Barbara. "The Quince's Delicious History." *The Washington Post.* 2008. http://www.washingtonpost.com/wp-dyn/content/article/2008/03/19/AR2008031900946.html

Danish Windmill. "Nordicware Old Fashion Krumkake Pan for Stove Top." *Danish Windmill.* 2011. http://www.danishwindmill.com/productcart/pc/Nordicware-Old-Fashion-Krumkake-Pan-for-Stove-Top-22p421.htm

Davidson, Alan and Tom Jaine. *The Oxford Companion To Food.* Oxford: Oxford University Press, 2006.

Day, Ivan. "Wafer Making." *Historic Food.* 2003. http://www.historicfood.com/Wafer.htm

Diamond Organics. "Fall and Winter

Fruit." *Diamond Organics.* 2010. https://www.diamondorganics.com/category/organic_fall_winter_fruit

Emerson, Brett. "The fruit that blushes when you cook it." *In Praise of Sardines.* 2005. http://inpraiseofsardines.typepad.com/blogs/2005/10/the_fruit_that_.html

Encyclopedia Brittanica. "Strawberry." *Encyclopedia Brittanica.* 2011. http://www.britannica.com/EBchecked/topic/568585/strawberry

Food Timeline. "FAQs: pie and pastry." *Food Timeline.* 2000. http://www.foodtimeline.org/foodpies.html

Gaudio, Monica. "A Tale of Two Tarts," *Gode Cookery.* 2009. http://www.godecookery.com/twotarts/twotarts.html

Ioppolo, G. (2006). Dramatists and their manuscripts in the age of Shakespeare, Jonson, Middleton and Heywood. New York: Routledge.

Ioppolo, G. (2010). "Early modern handwriting." In M. Hattaway, A New Companion to English Renaissance Literature and Culture, Volumes 1-2. West Sussex, UK: Blackwell Publishing, 177-189.

Kinnamon, N. J. (2008), Recent Studies in Renaissance English Manuscripts (1996–2006). English Literary Renaissance, 38: 356–383. doi: 10.1111/j.1475-6757.2008.00128.x

Markham, Gervase. *The English Housewife*, Michael Best, ed. 1986. Montreal: McGill-Queen's University Press.

Medieval Cookery. "Pie Crusts." *Medieval Cookery.* 2010. http://www.medieval-cookery.com/notes/piecrust.html

Mendelson, Sara and Crawford, Patricia. 1998. *Women in Early Modern England: 1550-1720.* Oxford: Oxford University Press.

Miller, Gretchen. "The making of an apple and orange tart." *The making of an apple and orange tart.* n.d. http://www.cs.cmu.edu/afs/andrew/org/Medieval/www/src/contributed/grm/AS/cooking/apple-orange-tarte.html

Murrell, John. *A Daily Exercise for Ladies and Gentlewomen...* London: widow Helme. 1617.

Parkes, M. B. (1959). A study of certain kinds of script used in England in the late fourteenth and the fifteenth centuries, and the origins of the Tudor Secretary hand. (Unpublished doctoral dissertation). University of Oxford, Hertford: United Kingdom.

Rolek, Barbara. "Crispy Wafer Cookies Recipe—Polish Waffle." *About.com.* 2011. http://easteuropeanfood.about.com/od/polishdesserts/r/wafercookies.htm

Schoonover, David E., ed. 1998. *Ladie Borlase's Receiptes Booke.* Iowa City: University of Iowa Press.

Thirsk, Joan. 2007. *Food in Early Modern England: Phases, Fads, Fashions 1500-1760.* London: Hambledon Continuum.

Touissant-Samat, Maguelonne. *History of Food.* 1992. Trans: Anthea Bell. Malden, MA: Blackwell Publishing.

Wolfe, H. (2007). Manuscripts and their Makers in the English Renaissance. Shakespeare Studies, 35, 211+. Retrieved from http://go.galegroup.com.proxy.lib.fsu.edu/ps/i.do?id=GALE%7CA171658498&v=2.1&u=tall85761&it=r&p=AONE&sw=w

calligraphy Julia Skinner

book photos Melody Dworak

special thanks Greg Prickman

for Candle Light Press:

cover Jeremy Smith

layout John Ira Thomas

About Candle Light Press

Candle Light Press exists to publish diverse and original works in both graphic and text formats. Our authors and artists all share a connection to the state of Iowa, where we first put our works into the world. From there, our books are available whevever books are sold. *Modernizing Markham* is our first scholarly text, the first of many to explore special topics in history and culture.

www.candlelightpress.com

candle
light
press ™

1470 Walker Way, Coralville, IA 52241
ding@candlelightpress.com

About Modern Markham Editions

Modern Markham editions are a series of books exploring the work of Gervase Markham, a prolific author of works on the orderly running of the home and attached lands. He was so prolific that he was often thought to be England's first "hackney" or "hack" writer. There is much of interest in his works; but without some translation of method and undating of definitions, this can be very difficult. The goal of this series of books is to make these methods available to modern readers as a matter of historical interest.

Other Books From Candle Light Press

And The Sky Turned White... by Carter Allen
(ISBN 0976605309)

Atlanta by Carter Allen (ISBN 0976605341)

Dub Trub: Our World Is In Danger Now! by Carter
Allen (ISBN 9780976605379)

Dub Trub 2: The Peacemakers by Carter Allen
(ISBN 0974314781)

Dub Trub 3: This Dangerous Game by Carter
Allen (ISBN 0976605317)

The Fairer Sex Volume 1 by John Ira Thomas
and Jeremy Smith (ISBN 0974314757)

The Fairer Sex Volume 2 by John Ira Thomas
and Jeremy Smith (ISBN 0976605325)

Leap Years by Ian Bennett (ISBN 097431479X)

Man is Vox: Barracudae by John Ira Thomas and
Carter Allen (ISBN 0974314722)

Man Is Vox: Paingels by John Ira Thomas
and Carter Allen (ISBN 0974314749)

Nightcrawlers by Michael Ayers and Will Grant
(ISBN 097660535X)

Numbers: A Tale Of Shades And Angels by
John Ira Thomas and Jeremy Smith (ISBN
0974314706)

The Scrounge Wuz Here! by Will Grant (ISBN 0974314765)

Zoo Force: Dear Eniko by John Ira Thomas and Jeremy Smith (ISBN 0974314714)

Zoo Force: BBQ by John Ira Thomas and Jeremy Smith (ISBN 0974314773)

Zoo Force: Bean And Nothingness by John Ira Thomas and Jeremy Smith (ISBN 0974314773)

Zoo Force: We Heart Libraries by John Ira Thomas and Jeremy Smith (ISBN 0976605368)